DATE DUE

4-20-17			

The Library Store   #47-0103

What are leaves?

by Kelley MacAulay

Crabtree Publishing Company

www.crabtreebooks.com

Author
Kelley MacAulay

Publishing plan research and development
Reagan Miller, Crabtree Publishing Company

Editorial director
Kathy Middleton

Editors
Reagan Miller, Crystal Sikkens

Proofreader
Kelly McNiven

Notes to adults
Reagan Miller

Photo research
Crystal Sikkens

Design
Ken Wright

**Production coordinator
and prepress technician**
Ken Wright

Print coordinator
Margaret Amy Salter

Photographs
Thinkstock: pages 14, 20, 23, 24 (spines)
Other images by Shutterstock

Library and Archives Canada Cataloguing in Publication

MacAulay, Kelley, author
        What are leaves? / Kelley MacAulay.

(Plants close-up)
Includes index.
Issued in print and electronic formats.
ISBN 978-0-7787-1287-9 (bound).--ISBN 978-0-7787-0017-3 (pbk.).--
ISBN 978-1-4271-9373-5 (pdf).--ISBN 978-1-4271-9369-8 (html)

        1. Leaves--Juvenile literature. I. Title. II. Series: Plants close-up

QK649.M23 2013   j581.4'8   C2013-904051-X
                                          C2013-904052-8

Library of Congress Cataloging-in-Publication Data

MacAulay, Kelley.
    What are leaves? / Kelley MacAulay.
        p. cm. -- (Plants close-up)
    Includes index.
    ISBN 978-0-7787-1287-9 (reinforced library binding) -- ISBN 978-0-7787-0017-3
(pbk.) -- ISBN 978-1-4271-9373-5 (electronic pdf) -- ISBN 978-1-4271-9369-8
(electronic html)
    1. Leaves--Juvenile literature. I. Title. II. Series: Plants close-up.

    QK649.M19 2013
    581.4'8--dc23
                                              2013023434

Crabtree Publishing Company

www.crabtreebooks.com   1-800-387-7650

Printed in Hong Kong/092013/BK20130703

**Published in Canada
Crabtree Publishing**
616 Welland Ave.
St. Catharines, Ontario
L2M 5V6

**Published in the United States
Crabtree Publishing**
PMB 59051
350 Fifth Avenue, 59th Floor
New York, New York 10118

**Published in the United Kingdom
Crabtree Publishing**
Maritime House
Basin Road North, Hove
BN41 1WR

**Published in Australia
Crabtree Publishing**
3 Charles Street
Coburg North
VIC 3058

Contents

Plants are alive

Leaves are parts of plants. Plants are living things. Living things grow and change.

Flowers, stems, and roots are also parts of plants. Each plant part has a job to do to help the plant stay alive and grow.

flower

leaves

stem

roots

Looking at leaves

simple leaf

leaflets

compound leaf

Most leaves are green. Some are called simple leaves. They are made of one part. Others are called compound leaves. They are made up of small parts called **leaflets**.

Not all leaves look the same. Some leaves are thick and waxy. Other leaves are thin and sharp like needles. Leaves from the same plant can be different sizes.

On the stem

Many plants have leaves that grow from **nodes**. A node is the place where a leaf comes out of a stem. **Buds** grow from the nodes on a stem. Buds are new leaves that have not yet opened.

bud

stem

node

Other plants have leaves that grow from **stalks**. Stalks grow from nodes and attach leaves to the stem. Maple tree leaves grow from stalks. Stalks bend easily in the wind.

stem

stalk

Leaves make food

Living things need food to stay alive and grow. Plants make their own food. They make food in their leaves using sunlight, air, and water.

Leaves take in sunlight and air to make food.
A plant's stem holds up the leaves to take in
the sunlight.

Sunlight and air

Different parts of a leaf help it get the sunlight, air, and water it needs to make food. The flat part of a leaf is called the **blade**. The blade takes in a lot of sunlight.

blade

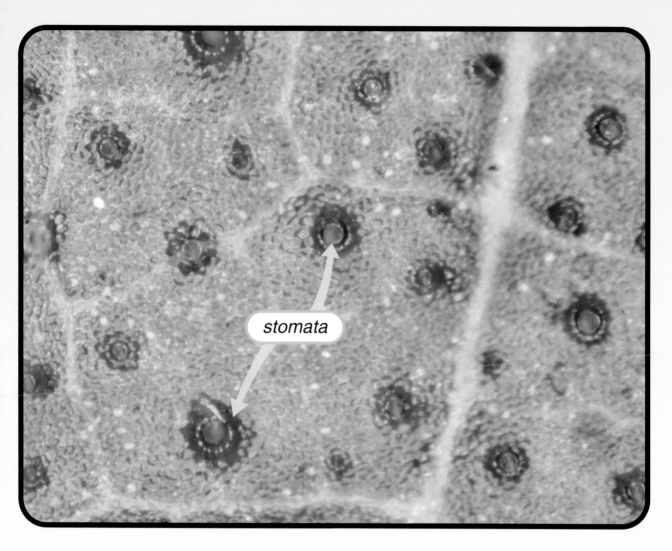

stomata

There are hundreds of holes on a leaf called **stomata**. The stomata are so small you cannot see them. The stomata let air into the leaf.

Moving water

Plants take in water through their roots. The water travels through the plant's stem to the leaves.

stem

roots

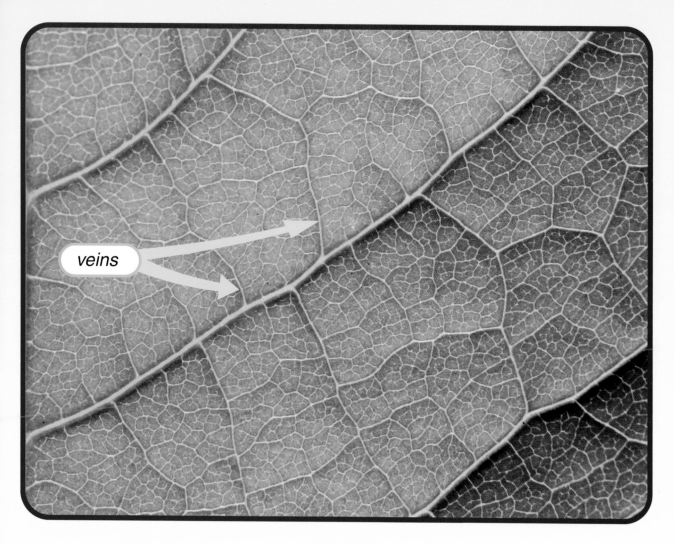

veins

Look closely at a leaf blade. There are lines in it called **veins**. Veins move water through the leaf.

Use and store

The food made in leaves is a kind of sugar called sap. The sap flows through the veins in the leaves to the stem. The stem moves the sap to other parts of the plant. The sap helps the plant stay healthy and grow.

Plants store some of the food they make. They store food in their leaves, stems, roots, and fruits. Fruits are other parts of plants.

leaves

fruit

stem

roots

Changing color

There are fewer hours of sunlight in autumn and winter than other seasons. With less sunlight, leaves cannot make food. Trees have to use their stored food to stay alive in autumn and winter.

Leaves turn yellow, orange, and red in autumn.
They fall to the ground after changing color.

New leaves grow

As winter ends, buds start to form on the trees. New leaves begin to grow from the buds. In spring, there is more sunlight. The leaves begin making new food for the plant.

Animals, such as deer and rabbits, eat the new green leaves of trees and other plants in spring.

Keeping safe

Plants need their leaves. Some plants have ways to protect their leaves against people and animals. Poison ivy is a plant that can give you an itchy rash if you touch its leaves.

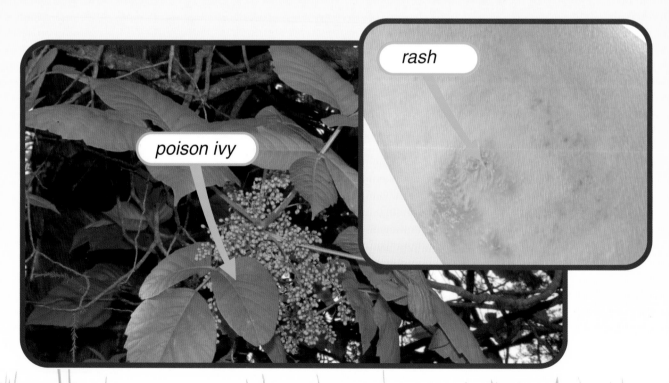

rash

poison ivy

spines

A holly tree has tiny sharp thorns called **spines** on its leaves. The spines hurt an animal's mouth if it tries to eat the leaves.

Words to know and Index

blade 12

buds 8, 20

leaflets 6

nodes 8

spines 23

stalks 9

stomata 13

veins 15

Notes for adults and an activity

Gather a variety of leaves from different kinds of plants.

• Have children sort the leaves using different criteria, such as sorting by shape, size, color, texture, type (simple and compound leaves) etc.

*Children should wear gloves to prevent reactions from leaves.

• Let children observe leaves through a magnifying glass. Have children identify the leaves' veins and stalks (if present)

• **Leaves on the Move!**

Explain to children that although plants cannot travel from place to place, some plant parts can move to help plants get what they need to survive. Place a houseplant on a window that gets a lot of sunlight. Have children observe the position of the leaves. Rotate the plant 90 degrees. The next day, have children observe the position of the leaves. The leaves will turn to face the sunlight.

Learning more

Books

Photosynthesis: Changing Sunlight into Food (Nature's Changes) by Bobbie Kalman. Crabtree Publishing Company (2005)

Amazing Plants (Amazing Science) by Sally Hewitt. Crabtree Publishing Company (2008)

Websites

The Great Plant Escape: Children team up with Detective LePlant to explore how a plant grows.
http://urbanext.illinois.edu/gpe/index.cfm

Trees are Terrific... Travels with Pierre: This engaging site from the University of Illinois examines how leaves change throughout the seasons.
http://urbanext.illinois.edu/trees1/index2.html